Artists Through the Ages

Paul Cézanne

Alix Wood

WINDMILL BOOKS

New York

Published in 2013 by Windmill Books, An Imprint of Rosen Publishing
29 East 21st Street, New York, NY 10010

Editor for Alix Wood Books: Eloise Macgregor
US Editor: Sara Antill
Designer: Alix Wood

Photo Credits: Cover, 1, 29, Paul Cézanne, Moscow, Puschkin-Museum © Artothek; 5 (top)
© Renaud Camus; 5 (bottom) © Tucker Collection; 7, Paul Cézanne, Washington DC, National
Gallery of Art, © NGA Images; 9, Paul Cézanne, Paris, Musée d'Orsay © Peter Willi - Artothek;
10 © Gaspard-Félix Tournachon; 11, Paul Cézanne, Sao Paolo, Museo de Arte © Imagno - Artothek;
12-13, Paul Cézanne, Munich, Neue Pinakothek © Artothek; 14-15, Paul Cézanne, © Christie's
Images Ltd - Artothek; 17, Paul Cézanne, London, Courtauld Institute © Imagno - Artothek;
19, Paul Cézanne, Zürich, Fondation E.G. Bührle Collection © Hans Hinz - Artothek; 20-21, Paul
Cézanne, Moscow, Puschkin-Museum © Artothek; 23, Paul Cézanne, St. Petersburg, Hermitage
© Artothek; 24-25 © nga, Ailsa Mellon Bruce Collection; 27, Paul Cézanne, Moscow, Puschkin-
Museum © Hans Hinz - Artothek; 28, © Dianne Pike; 3, 4 (bottom), 6, 8, 16, 22, 30 © Shutterstock

Library of Congress Cataloging-in-Publication Data

Wood, Alix.
 Paul Cézanne / by Alix Wood.
    p. cm. — (Artists through the ages)
 Includes index.
 ISBN 978-1-61533-619-7 (library binding) — ISBN 978-1-61533-625-8 (pbk.) —
ISBN 978-1-61533-626-5 (6-pack)
 1. Cézanne, Paul, 1839–1906—Juvenile literature. 2. Painters—France—Biography—
Juvenile literature. I. Title.
 ND553.C33W66 2013
 759.4—dc23
 [B]

2012020269

Manufactured in the United States of America

CPSIA Compliance Information: Batch #BW13WM: For Further Information contact Windmill Books, New York, New York at 1-866-478-0556

Contents

Who Was Cézanne?

Paul Cézanne was a French artist. He was born in Aix-en-Provence in the south of France in 1839. His father was a rich banker. Cézanne had two younger sisters, Marie and Rose. When he was ten, Cézanne went to Saint Joseph school and enjoyed drawing. His father wanted him to work in his bank when he was older.

Paul Cézanne

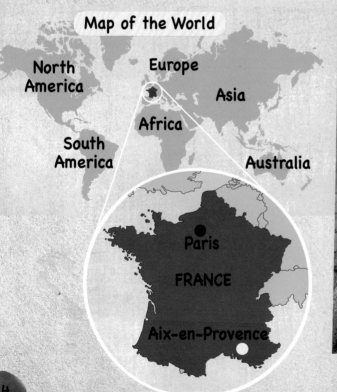

Map of the World

North America

Europe

Asia

Africa

South America

Australia

Paris

FRANCE

Aix-en-Provence

A typical narrow street in Aix-en-Provence, France.

Cézanne's family moved to this house when Paul was 20 years old. Cézanne lived here after his parents died, too.

Clever friends

Cézanne went to college when he was 13, and met Émile Zola and Baptistin Baille. The three were known at school as "the three **inseperables**" because they were always together. Zola went on to become a famous writer, and Baille became a **professor**.

Émile Zola

The Young Cézanne

When Cézanne was at college, he also took classes at a local drawing school. When his friend Émile Zola moved to Paris to study, he wrote letters to Cézanne. Cézanne wanted to join his friend in Paris and paint there. Cézanne's father did not want him to be an artist, though. Cézanne failed his school exams, but then passed them in November with a grade "assez bien," which means "good enough"!

Cézanne loved to walk in the French countryside and paint the things that he saw.

The Artist's
Father Reading
L'Événement,
1866

Cézanne in Paris

Eventually Cézanne's father gave in and let him go to Paris, with a little bit of money to live on. His first stay in Paris only lasted six months. He was unhappy with his paintings, got depressed, and went back home. After a year working with his father, though, he returned to Paris.

Paris was a bustling city in the 1860s. The area around Montmartre where Cézanne stayed was home to many of the young **Impressionist** painters. Originally a small village on the edge of Paris, it became part of Paris in 1860 as the city grew. This area of Paris is still popular with artists today.

A photograph of Montmartre today

The Paris Countryside

Cézanne would go to paint in the villages around Paris. Auvers-sur-Oise was a favorite place for many Paris artists. Cézanne liked to paint the old cottages. He later moved there to live. The painting above is one of the few paintings Cézanne signed.

Rejection

Success was hard to find. Cézanne failed the exam to get into the best art school in Paris. Even the school's gallery, the Salon, would not show his paintings. The Salon rejected Cézanne's paintings every year. After nearly 20 years of trying, in 1882 they at last accepted the **portrait** of his father (the painting on page 7).

Cézanne made friends with the painter Camille Pissarro. Pissarro introduced Cézanne to Impressionist painters Édouard Manet and Edgar Degas. They all thought Cézanne was odd. Cézanne once wouldn't shake hands with Manet, saying it was because he (Cézanne) hadn't washed for eight days.

The painter Édouard Manet

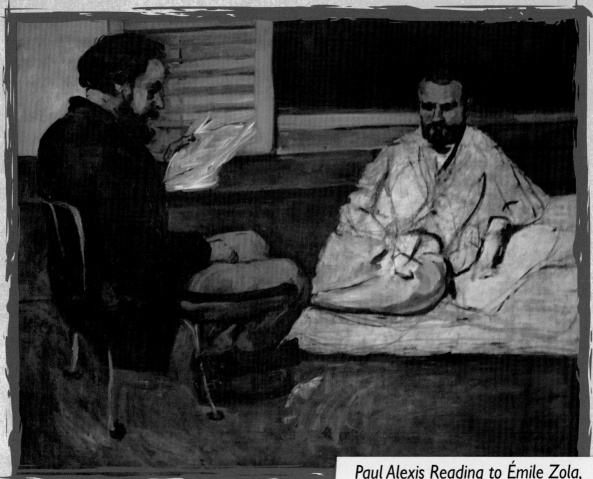

Paul Alexis Reading to Émile Zola,
painted around 1869

Dark Paintings

Cézanne's paintings from this time used dark colors and a lot of black. They were sometimes depressing and violent. The painting above of his friends Alexis and Zola was done at the end of this dark period. Zola and Alexis once stopped a sword fight between the artist Édouard Manet and an **art critic** who'd insulted his work!

Simple Shapes

Cézanne liked to paint solid shapes. An apple's shape was very important to him. He painted the shapes with strong, simple brushstrokes. When Cézanne was alive, people said he wasn't a very good painter. He did not paint like most other people painted.

Hold a ruler along the front of the table top in the painting to the right. Do the two sides of the table match up? No. Cézanne liked to draw objects from different **angles** in the same painting.

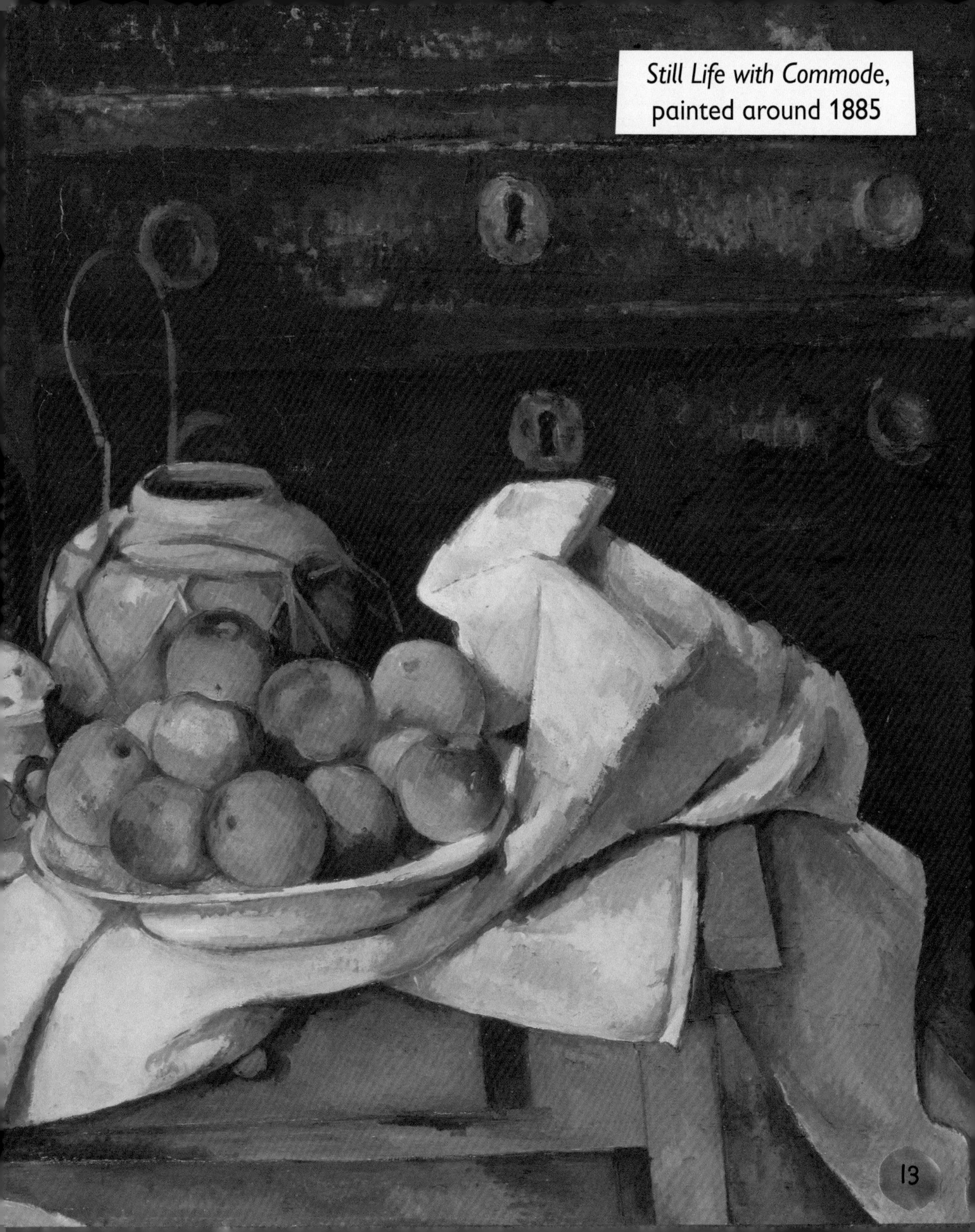

Still Life with Commode,
painted around 1885

Painting Trips

Cézanne's friend Camille Pissarro was nine years older than him, and a little like a father figure. Cézanne enjoyed learning Pissarro's Impressionist style. They would go into the countryside and paint together. Cézanne's way of painting changed to be a little less dark. He began to paint more **landscapes**.

Impressionism

Impressionists like to paint an impression, rather than a detailed, realistic painting. They use dabs of primary colors (red, blue, and yellow) to give the effect of light.

The Rooftops Of L'Estaque, 1883–1885

Postimpressionism

Before photographs, the main reason to buy a painting was to have a realistic picture of something you liked, such as a portrait of your dog or a pretty place you'd visited. **Postimpressionist** painters like Cézanne began to put feelings into their art instead.

Cézanne would sometimes take hours to do a single brush stroke. A still life took Cézanne one hundred working sessions, a portrait took him around one hundred and fifty sessions. He rarely signed his paintings because he felt they were not completely finished. Cézanne worked on the still life on the opposite page over a long time, and he moved around it as he painted.

What's a Postimpressionist?

"Post" means "after," so Postimpressionists came after Impressionist painters and had a new style.

Still Life with Plaster Cast, painted around 1894

17

Family Life

Cézanne met Marie-Hortense Fiquet. They married and had a son named Paul. Cézanne kept his wife and child secret from his father at first. His father found out and stopped sending him money. Things were hard for Cézanne. Eventually his father felt sorry and gave his family some more money, and he built Cézanne a **studio** to paint in at the family house.

Madame Cézanne

In all the paintings of Cézanne's wife she never looks very happy. But remember that she would have had to sit for him over 100 times. She probably was getting a little bored! After his friend Ambroise Vollard had done 115 sittings for a portrait, Cézanne famously said "I am not altogether displeased with the shirt-front."

The Artist's Wife with a Fan, 1878–1888

19

Back in Provence

When Cézanne's father died, the family moved to his father's big house in Aix-en-Provence. His wife's brother had a house nearby with a view of Mont Sainte-Victoire.

The Sainte-Victoire mountain was one of Cézanne's favorite subjects and he painted it over 60 times. Cézanne liked the rugged forms and painted the same scene from many different angles. He would use bold blocks of color to show the unusual rock shapes of the mountains. To him the mountain was everything that was missing from Impressionist paintings. It was solid and **permanent**.

Mont Sainte-Victoire, 1885

The Pipe Smoker

Cézanne painted pictures of the workers who helped at his large house at Jas de Bouffan. He did paintings of them playing cards or relaxing and smoking their pipes. He found the men as solid and unchanging as the mountain he loved to paint.

The gardens at Jas de Bouffan

Who Was He?

The man in the painting on the opposite page was Cézanne's gardener, Paulin Paulet. He appears in many of Cézanne's paintings, including all of his card player paintings, along with a farm worker called le père Alexandre.

The Pipe Smoker, painted around 1891

23

Changing Times

In the same year that his father died, Cézanne's old friend Émile Zola wrote a book about an unsuccessful artist. Everyone thought the book was about Cézanne and this broke their friendship.

As young boys, Cézanne, Zola, and Baille would often go to the Arc river to swim. As an adult, Cézanne often painted pictures of bathers and rivers, which reminded him of happier times.

Riverbank, painted around 1895

His Later Life

For many years Cézanne's paintings were unknown. In 1895, Ambroise Vollard, a Paris art dealer, arranged a show of Cézanne's work. By 1904, Cézanne was featured in a major official exhibition, and by the time of his death in 1906 he had become well known. During his last years many younger artists traveled to Aix-en-Provence to watch him at work and to learn from him.

At the age of 67, Cézanne was caught in a heavy rainstorm while working on a landscape. Cold and wet, he started walking home, but collapsed. He was found some time later by a man driving a laundry cart. Eight days later Cézanne died of **pneumonia**. He was buried at the old cemetery in his beloved hometown of Aix-en-Provence.

Mardi Gras

Harlequin and Pierrot were characters in a type of comedy show that was popular in France. In this painting, Harlequin (right) is played by Cézanne's son, Paul, and Pierrot (left) is Paul's friend Louis Guillaume.

Pierrot and Harlequin (Mardi Gras), 1888

Cézanne's Legacy

Paul Cézanne influenced many artists with his new ideas and ways of painting. The way he simplified painting into basic shapes influenced the Cubist painters that followed. His subject matter, and his use of color, inspired many artists, such as Henri Matisse and Pablo Picasso. He influenced Expressionist painters, too, who wanted to put feeling into their work, like Cézanne did.

His paintings were exhibited in Paris the year after his death. Cézanne struggled to earn money from his painting while he was alive, but now his paintings sell for millions of dollars.

In Aix-en-Provence this statue by sculptor Gabriël Sterk commemorates Paul Cézanne.

PAUL CEZANNE
1839 · 1906

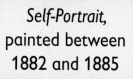

Self-Portrait,
painted between
1882 and 1885

Glossary

angle (ANG-gul)
The space between two lines or planes that come together at a point.

art critic
(ART KRIH-tik)
A person who judges works of art as their job.

Impressionist
(im-PREH-shuh-nist)
Relating to a style of art in which the subject is not as important as how the artist uses color and tone.

inseperables
(in-SEH-puh-ruh-bulz)
Something that is impossible to separate.

landscapes
(LAND-skayps)
Pictures of natural scenery.

permanent
(PER-muh-nint)
Lasting or intended to last for a very long time.

pneumonia
(noo-MOH-nya)
A disease in which the
lungs become inflamed
and fill with thick liquid.

portrait (POR-tret)
A picture of a person
usually showing the face.

Postimpressionist
(pohst-im-PREH-shuh-
nist) An artist who rejects

the naturalism of the
impressionists and uses
form and color in more
expressive ways.

professor (preh-FEH-ser)
A teacher especially of
the highest rank at a
college or university.

studio (STOO-dee-oh)
The working place of
an artist.

Websites

For web resources related to the
subject of this book, go to:
www.windmillbooks.com/weblinks
and select this book's title.

Read More

Burleigh, Robert. *Paul Cézanne: A Painter's Journey.* New York: Harry N. Abrams, 2006.

Mis, Melody S. *Paul Cézanne.* Meet the Artist. New York: PowerKids Press, 2008.

Spence, David. *The Impressionists: Monet, Cézanne, Renoir, Degas.* Royal Tunbridge Wells, UK: TickTock Books Ltd., 2010.

Index